√ dup

D1236126

FAMILY MATTERS

# EARLY
# LEARNING
# GAMES

Distributed by
**STERLING PUBLISHING CO., INC.**
387 Park Avenue South

FAMILY MATTERS

✓

# EARLY LEARNING GAMES

**SHIRLEY STAINES**

**WARD LOCK**

First published 1990 by Ward Lock
Artillery House, Artillery Row, London SW1P 1RT, England

A Cassell imprint

© Text and illustrations Ward Lock Limited 1990

Line drawings by Tony Randell

Text filmset in Garamond Book ITC
by Columns of Reading
Printed and bound in Scotland by
William Collins & Co. Glasgow

**British Library Cataloguing in Publication Data**
Staines, Shirley
   Early learning games.   –  (Family matters)
   1. Children's games
   I. Title  II. Series
   790.1'922

   ISBN 0–7063–6771–5

# CONTENTS

# CONTENTS

# INTRODUCTION

Here is a book full of games and activities for you and your children to enjoy together. Most I have played with my children, some I discovered while researching this book.

There is no mystery to learning through play. When children play they cannot help but learn and develop. Some activities, however, are more valuable to development than others. I hope the main value of this book will be as a source of good ideas and whichever page you turn to you will find at least one suggestion which inspires you into 'having a go'!

There are no rules on how to use this book – work through it, select ideas at random or, and I think this is probably the best method, suggest a few activities to the children and let them choose!

## A FEW FACTS AND GUIDELINES

All the games and activities in this book have been tried, tested and they work. Over the years, I've experienced failure with biscuits that didn't set, collages that wouldn't stick and paper frogs that refused to jump despite manic attempts to 'tickle' them across the floor with a rolled-up newspaper.

A friend trying some of the activities described them as 'creator friendly'.

This book is aimed at pre-school children but to give specific age guides would be futile. Children develop at different rates, and a child who is forward in one area may not necessarily be competent in all skills. The four-year-old who can count backwards perfectly may well wield a paste brush with all the dexterity of a gorilla.

Do try and turn a 'deaf ear' to other mothers talking about their 'gifted' children. Keep reassuring yourself with the fact that statistically, yours cannot be the only below average child.

If a child is interested and enjoying the activity, he or she will be trying hard to please, so do give lots of praise and encouragement. Resist the temptation to interfere, correct or perfect. In the beginning, Daddy will be painted with his arm growing out of his head and probably with a navel the size of a saucer but stick the picture on the wall and be delighted with it regardless!

The 'learning' value of a game may not always be obvious but don't fall into the trap of only offering 'educational' games and toys to your child. Even digging a hole in the garden and splashing about in the bath water can help develop senses and vocabulary.

Keep talking! Children aren't born knowing the difference between big and small, where their elbows and eyebrows are or that to 'stick' means to join one thing to another. Get into the habit of thinking aloud, describe what you are doing, discuss textures, compare sizes or temperatures, make an effort to chat and point out things of interest.

I've tried to keep material expenses down to a minimum but it does make sense to become a hoarder. Save food trays, ice cream boxes, stiff card. Don't throw away unwanted wallpaper and get on friendly terms with a computer operator and commandeer used computer paper. It is clean on one side and makes perfect drawing and painting paper.

Some children like to paint over their pictures, flatten their models, knock down bricks – don't panic – it is simply a way of showing independence. He or she drew it, modelled it, built it and therefore has the right to destroy it. Of course, it could be less complicated than that – you could simply have a prospective demolition worker on your hands.

Enjoy yourselves. Children love to play. It comes naturally to them. They don't need cajoling or bribing – they do it automatically! I used to bribe my children to take medicine, holding the spoon in one hand and a sweet in the other. Thinking back, they would have gladly swallowed the sickly-sweet, delicious medicine with or without the bribe. The same applies to playing, it isn't a punishment – it is simply to be enjoyed. Have fun!

# PAINTING, PRINTING AND DRAWING

All children make pictures using whatever materials are available to them – sticks in sand, fingers in spilt drinks or carefully laid out paints and paper. An art session doesn't demand a lot of organizing, it can be as simple as supplying a pile of computer paper and a couple of wax crayons. But it is an invaluable activity for developing many skills including co-ordination, recognition and vocabulary.

## PAINTING

Don't expect to recognize first painting efforts, just stand back and enjoy watching the gradual progress from colourful blobs to masterpieces.

★ *CLOTHING* Invest in long-sleeved painting overalls or use an old shirt. In the summer, when arms are bare, the supermarket carrier bags with shaped handles make good disposable sleeveless overalls – head through the top, arm through each handle. Do take care to supervise activities using carrier bags at all times for safety reasons.

★ *STAINS* Powder paints wash out of clothes more

## PAINTS

**READY-MIXED PAINTS**
These are very convenient but expensive – water them down to make them go further.

**POWDER PAINTS**
These are fairly inexpensive, very versatile and can be mixed to any consistency. Children enjoy mixing them themselves. Mix with non-fungicidal made-up wallpaper paste or starch for a thick, creamy paint.

**BLOCK PAINTS**
These usually come in palettes of six or more colours, and so give an instant and inexpensive supply of different colours. They are not suitable for all types of craft work, and young children find cleaning the brush between colours difficult and frustrating.

**BRUSHES**
Until the fine artist in your child develops, chubby, shorthandled brushes are the most satisfying to use. Finish each painting session with a 'wash-out' – washing the brushes in warm soapy water. Most children enjoy this chore.

**CRAYONS**
Choose short, stubby crayons for young children – thin crayons break easily. Lots of activities involve using the side of the crayon, so remove any protective paper.

easily than poster paints. Block paints are extremely difficult to remove. However, all three will wash out far more easily if you add just a dot of washing-up liquid to the paint or the mixing water before using.

★ *AVOIDING SPILLS* Spillproof paint pots save tempers as well as paints. You can make them out of plastic bottles but shop versions have air-tight lids which keep the paint 'usable' for ages. If paint does dry out, add a few drops of hot water, leave for a while and blend in the dried paint.

★ *PAPER* Paper doesn't have to be square, plain and white. Offer coloured paper, textured wallpaper and try cutting it into circular or triangular shapes for a change.

## LIFESIZE PORTRAITS

This activity takes plenty of time and paint but is very popular, and I still occasionally unroll the picture of my daughter, painted when she was five.

*Unwanted rolls of wallpaper or lining paper*
*Crayons*
*Paints*
*Brushes*

1. Cut a length of wallpaper at least as long as the child is tall.
2. Ask the child to lie down on top of the wallpaper (unpatterned side up). Using a black crayon draw around the child's outline.
3. Talk about what colours and buttons, the child is wearing, the colour of hair, eyes, and the other features, and fill in the outline using the correct colour paints.
4. Children rarely have any real

*Another project idea. On a fine day supply a bucket of clean water and a very large brush and let the children 'paint' the garden fence, the patio, the shed – what marvellous, harmless freedom and fun!*

idea of their size, so do hang these models on the wall where they can illustrate actual measurements and how they compare with other things.

## COLOUR MIXING

*Paper*
*Blue crayon*
*Yellow crayon*
*Brown crayon*

1. Draw outline of a tree and a big round sun for child to colour in.
2. Use blue crayon for sky, yellow for sun and brown for trunk.
3. Explain how blue and yellow make green and prove it by using the blue and yellow crayons to colour the tree green.

☆ Experiment to see how many colours you can make by combining two or more different colours.

☆ Ask questions like, 'I haven't got a green crayon how can I colour the grass?' to test colour knowledge.

## PRINTING

Printing is an exciting activity because it produces

such effective and unpredictable results. It is an ideal way of introducing and explaining about shapes.

*Small, shallow food trays (from supermarket packaged meat or vegetables)*
*Piece of thin sponge or foam (to fit in the base of the tray)*
*Paint*
*Corks, cotton reels and brushes for making prints*
*Paper*

1. Line the bottom of the tray with the foam or sponge.
2. Pour a couple of tablespoons of paint over the top and let the sponge or foam soak it up.
3. Press objects into paint pad and transfer on to paper to make random patterns.

## SOME EASY IDEAS

▶ Show how pictures can be built up, brick prints for houses, cork prints for the sun, etc.

▶ Cut carrots, mushrooms, onions and sprouts in half, the cut surfaces give good patterned prints. Whittle away the cut surface of a potato into an interesting shape for printing.

▶ Paint a bus, give it onion print wheels or a face with a mushroom print nose. Cut out a paper giraffe and zebra and give them carrot spots and peg print stripes.

### BUTTERFLIES

*Paper*
*Scissors*
*Paint and brushes*

1. Fold a sheet of paper in half, draw one butterfly wing along fold. Cut through both thicknesses of paper and you should end up with one complete butterfly. Make up a card template and allow older children

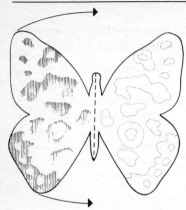

to draw around and cut out their own butterfly.

2. Open out the butterfly and paint just one wing. Use bright colours and plenty of paint.

3. Fold the butterfly in half again and press down firmly. Just like blotting paper and ink, the clean side will 'blot' the paint and when the paper is unfolded a beautiful butterfly with matching wings will emerge.

☆ Try painting half a house, a tree or a face and folding the paper over to complete the picture – children find it great fun just painting one eye, etc. and it gives a good opportunity to discuss how many ears, etc., we have and where they are.

☆ Sure as night follows day, if you blink you will find both sides of the paper painted so either cover one side or tuck one behind the other.

| BUBBLE PICTURES |
| --- |

Experiment using plain water to ensure blowing isn't confused with sucking before you try this activity.

*A beaker or tub approximately half full of thinnish paint*

*A mean tablespoon of washing-up liquid*

*Straws*

*Lightweight paper*

1. Stir the washing-up liquid into the paint.

2. Using the straw, blow bubbles into the paint until they rise to the top of the beaker.

3. When the bubbles are about to overflow, gently lay a sheet of paper on top of them. The bubbles make lovely patterns on the paper.

> *Children love watching bubbles climb and overflow. It's a bit messy but just as much enjoyment is gained from blowing and watching the bubbles as from making the prints.*

☆ While the straws are out, try spooning a big blob of paint on to a piece of paper. Blow down a drinking straw, moving it around the paper to make weird and wonderful patterns, and discuss what you think the shapes look like.

### FINGER PAINTING

This is a very messy activity so make sure that clothing, floor and surrounding streets are protected. A window wiper, with either a sponge or rubber blade is ideal for keeping the paint away from the edges of the table.

Some children hate getting mucky fingers. Encourage them to join in by offering pretty colours and by letting them use paste scrapers, brushes, or spoons if they prefer.

*Powder paint*
*Wallpaper paste (do check that it doesn't contain a fungicide or starch)*
*A tray, old baking sheet or wipe-clean table*

> Write your child's name in the paint and take a print by laying paper over pressing down firmly. The print will be in 'mirror' image, show how it looks 'right' when held in front of the mirror.

1. Simply place spoonfuls of paste and paint on surface for the child to mix together and create ever-changing patterns and pictures.
2. Have plenty of paper handy to take prints of patterns and handprints.

## MORE UNUSUAL PROJECTS

When the rain pours and everyone is bored, it's good to have something 'special' to do. The following ideas are good for brightening up an hour or more.

### MAGIC MESSAGES

*Paper*
*White household candles*
*Black paint, mixed thinly*
*Paintbrush*

1. Using a candle and pressing firmly, write a name or draw a picture on the paper.
2. Brush the thin black paint across the paper to reveal the message, name or picture. Older children will enjoy sending secret messages to friends, younger children will simply enjoy surprising somebody with a picture.

☆ Make a game out of trying to guess what the word or picture is before it is completely revealed.

### FLOWERS WHICH CHANGE COLOUR

*White carnations (other flowers and colours work, but not so effectively)*
*Ink, food colouring*
*Paint*
*Water*

1. Take the flower and slit the stem lengthways to the head/bloom.
2. Make up a strong solution of ink, paint or food colouring and water and place in a small vase.
3. Place the stem in the vase and after a few hours, as it takes up the coloured water, the flower will begin to change colour.
4. Try placing only one side of the stem in the dye – only the corresponding side of the flower

will change colour. Put the two halves of the stem in different coloured dyes for a multicoloured flower.

5. Nothing will happen for an hour or more, so this is an activity to leave and return to later.

6. Use this activity as an opportunity to explain the different parts of a flower – stem, stamen, petal – and how they grow.

## LEAF AND BARK RUBBINGS

*Chubby wax crayons*
*Thin paper*
*Selection of leaves and barks*

> Paint over and around leaves positioned on a sheet of paper, remove the leaves and you will be left with interesting leaf stencils.

1. Place leaves smooth side down on table and cover with a sheet of paper.

2. Using the side of the crayon, rub over the paper until the pattern of the leaves shows through.

3. For bark rubbings hold the paper firmly over the bark and rub over the surface with the crayon.

☆ See how many different barks you can take rubbings from. Stick them in a scrapbook pairing bark and leaf rubbings.

☆ Take rubbings from an endless variety of everyday objects: coins, stones, carpets, cane furniture, fabric....

## SNOW PICTURES

*2 cups of soap flakes*
*¼ cup water*
*Black or dark paper*
*Paste scraper*

1. Whisk together the soap flakes and water until they look like whipped cream (you can use an electric mixer for this).

2. Using a paste scraper, paint a snow scene, snowman, snow pattern – whatever you like.

3. Try drawing or painting a picture and adding snow on afterwards. The soap snow dries crisp.

☆ Soap snow can also be used to make models. Mould and model on a damp surface and keep hands moist to prevent sticking but not too wet or else this 'expensive' snow will melt away.

☆ Soap snow can be stored indefinitely in an airtight container. When you want to use it just whisk in a little more water to make it pliable again.

---

Light is made up of lots of colours but only when light rays are broken up by raindrops do we actually see those colours in the form of a rainbow.

You can make your own rainbow by placing a glass of water on the edge of the window sill and letting the sunlight shine through it on to a sheet of paper below: an instant rainbow.

Paint a rainbow – the colours are violet, indigo, blue, green, yellow, orange and red.

---

# MODELLING AND COLLAGES

Even the youngest child enjoys sticking pretty pictures on to a piece of paper or cardboard, while older children can be amazingly imaginative and produce wonderful models from junk, dough or scraps of paper and fabric.

## MODELLING

Introduce a child to modelling dough and be prepared for a diet of playdough 'cherry buns' and other delicacies for the next year!

As soon as a child stops eating everything found in his or her hand, he or she can be given a 'lump' of dough to roll, squidge and very occasionally make something indentifiable with. Encourage the child to experiment with shapes and methods.

### PLAYDOUGH

If you have flour in your cupboard and water you have the ingredients to make a batch of playdough — simply mix the two together. Adding salt prevents the dough from 'going off' and a little cooking oil keeps the dough pliable. Use powder paint or food colouring to colour the playdough.

## Basic Playdough Recipe

| | |
|---|---|
| *3 cups plain flour* | Mix together the dry ingredients. |
| *1 cup salt* | Add the oil and food colouring if |
| *Approximately 2 cups water* | used. |
| *2 tablespoons cooking oil* | Add enough water to make a soft |
| *Paint or food colouring* | but not sticky dough. |

☆ Do let the children measure, mix and knead the dough themselves. Making it is an absorbing and enjoyable activity in itself.

☆ Don't inhibit children's creative talents by insisting that 'something' is made with playdough. Children are often satisfied simply 'squidging' the dough, rolling out sausages and seeing how far it stretches before breaking.

## MODELLING PASTRY

This simple to make pastry dough can be 'fired' in a low oven until hard and when cool, painted and varnished. It is ideal for making small models, plaques, pictures, jewellery and play food for the Wendy House or shop.

## Modelling Pastry Recipe

| | |
|---|---|
| *2 cups plain flour* | Mix together the flour and salt. |
| *1 cup salt* | Gradually, add water until you |
| *Approximately ½ cup water* | have a soft 'workable' dough. |

## PERSONALIZED TEDDY DOOR PLAQUES

*Modelling pastry*
*Paint*
*Double-sided sticky pad*
  *(for handing plaque)*

1. Roll out the pastry until it is approximately 5 mm ( ¼ in) thick. (It will rise slightly during cooking).

2. Using a stiff card template as a guide, help the child to cut out a teddy bear shape. It should be

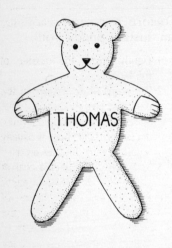

around 18 cm (7 in) tall with a tummy fat enough to write the child's name across.

3. Lay ted on a lightly-greased baking tray and bake in a low oven for two to three hours until hard.

4. When cool, paint the front. Leave to dry, then add eyes, ears, nose, paws and claws.

5. Finally, an adult should paint or felt tip 'name of child's room' across ted's middle.

6. Place a double-sided sticky pad on the back, and stick him on the bedroom door.

---

*If you didn't feel confident enough to make a teddy template, use whatever pastry cutters you have – Gingerbread men are ideal. Jewellery, model animals for farms and play food for shops can all be made easily using the small pastry cutters you can buy from most toy shops.*

---

★ *PAPIER MÂCHÉ* A crude version of papier mâché – coating a 'mould' with layers of newspaper and paste can be adopted to make all kinds of pots, masks and models.

★ *JUNK MODELS* 'One person's empty box is another mind's paddle steamer!' Children adore making models out of rubbish – boxes, wrapping paper, cellophane, corrugated card, cardboard inner tubes, etc., all make good modelling materials.

---

*A good PVA glue is essential for junk modelling. Earthquakes and hurricanes cannot be compared with the upset caused by a collapsed junk model!*

---

## PAPIER MÂCHÉ PENCIL POTS

These take a day to dry before they are ready for painting so don't promise an 'instant pencil pot!'.

*Wallpaper paste (without fungicide)*
*Newspaper shredded into pieces approximately 1 × 3 cm (½ × 1¼ in). Children love this part of the preparation*
*A plastic beaker or the bottom half of a washing-up liquid bottle*
*Pasting brush*
*Paint*

1. Lightly grease the outside of the beaker.
2. Dip strips of newspaper in the paste and give the beaker a coat of newspaper overlapping where necessary. Adult help is usually required with this first layer.
3. Now give the beaker a coat of paste, stick on a coat of paper and continue with layers of paste and paper until the beaker has about six coats of newspaper. Press down any turned up corners and finish with a layer of paper.
4. Leave the pot to dry overnight before gently easing the beaker out of its paper overcoat.
5. Paint or decorate the pot as you wish.

☆ Using inflated balloons and plates as bases you can make all sorts of models and masks with papier mâché.

*Door plaques and pen holders may seem ambitious projects but they only call upon basic skills. If the children enjoyed making them, it doesn't matter if their efforts resemble doughnuts and squashed cans.*

## COLLAGES

Even children who find drawing difficult enjoy making collages: filling in outlines, building up pictures or simply making patterns. Don't restrict collages just to paper and fabric. Coloured sand, twigs, buttons, crushed and washed egg shells are all suitable.

Let the family eat pasta for a month while you collect the various shapes. The shells, twirls, tubes and stars can be coloured with paint or food colouring. Choose small shapes, as the larger ones tend not to stick.

### SWAN HAND PRINT COLLAGE

*White paper (tissue or crêpe if you have some, plain drawing paper if you don't)*

*Scissors*

*Paste and brush*

*Sheet of blue paper for background*

*Orange and black crayons for finishing off*

1. Draw the outline of a large swan on the coloured paper.
2. Show the child how to draw around a hand. The fingers should be closed. These hand shapes are going to become the swan's feathers.
3. Cut out twenty or more feathers – it doesn't matter if they are not so much cut out as chewed up – 'practice will eventually make perfect!'
4. Sticking just one of each feather and overlapping them to look like the real things, fill in the outline of the swan.
5. Finish off by colouring in the beak and eyes. Using green paper, you could cut out more hand shapes – this time with fingers open to resemble pond weed.

Use hand and finger for fish, peacock tails and trees in collages.

## VASE OF FLOWERS COLLAGE

*A sheet of paper*
*Scraps of patterned wallpaper or wrapping paper*
*Straws*
*Contrasting paper, fabric for vase*
*Scraps of tissue paper*
*Paste and brush*

1. Cut out the twelve or more petal shapes from the wall or wrapping paper and a vase shape from the contrasting paper. Give the children a card template of the vase and oval petal shapes and let them draw and cut out their own.
2. Stick the vase shape near the bottom of the sheet of paper.
3. Position and stick three or four straws just above the vase to resemble stems.
4. Using the straws as guides, stick the petals in place arranging four or five petals around the top of each stem to make up the blooms.
5. Finish off with a small 'ball' of tissue paper in the centre of each flower.

## FAMILY TREE COLLAGE

*Some fine twigs broken into pieces about 2 cm (¾ in) long*
*Lengths of spaghetti or straws for the trunk*
*A sheet of paper*
*Paste and brush*
*'Headshot' photographs of close family: grandparents, parents, and brothers and sisters*

1. Make a tree trunk on the sheet of paper with the straws or spaghetti. Alternatively, try making a bark rubbing for the tree trunk instead of the straws or spaghetti.
2. Using the fine twigs, help the child place the 'branches' either side of the trunk. There should be as many branches as members of family to be included.

3. Talk about how the family is made up and, beginning with grandparents, stick the photographs or pictures at the end of the branches in their correct positions.

☆ If you don't want to destroy the family album for the family tree, help your child to draw faces of close family and cut those out.

☆ Keep the family tree to close members of family. Children are often amazed to learn that grandparents are Mummy and Daddy's parents.

☆ Discuss how members of the family look alike, are the same size, have the same eye and hair colouring, etc. If the child resembles the milkman best find another topic for discussion!!!

## SHAPE COLLAGE

*A sheet of paper*
*Some coloured paper cut into various shapes: circles, ovals, squares, ... (this is a job for an adult as the shapes need to be recognizable)*
*Paste and brush*

1. An adult should draw the simple outline of a house, boat, or person using shapes as templates: squares for houses, rectangles for doors and so on.
2. Help the child to find the correct shapes to fit and stick on the outline.
3. Discuss the shapes and with them build up a picture. Teddy can be built-up from ovals, circles and semi-circles, pigs from circles, ovals and triangles.
4. If your drawing usually requires explanations, these 'shape' pictures are great – and you

can 'fool' yourself into believing they have to be simple for the children's sake!

## 3-D PICTURES

*Lids from margarine tubs or meat and vegetable trays*
*Greetings cards*
*Double-sided sticky tape*
*Paste or Blu-Tack*

> *If you come across any inexpensive cotton wool buy it! It is invaluable for craft work and makes an ideal collage material for sheep pictures, snow scenes, anything. Coloured cotton wool balls are particularly useful for craftwork.*

1. Line the base of the lid or tray 'frame' with a piece of plain card or suitable 'background' picture. Use paste for cardboard 'frames', Blu-Tack for plastic.
2. Help the child to select shapes, animals and people from the pictures on the front of the greetings cards. Cut these out. Draw boxes around fiddly shapes as a guide for young children.
3. Decide whereabouts on the background the 'cut-outs' look best and press them into place using sticky pads.

## DESIGNER DOLLS

*A sheet of paper*
*Scraps of fabric and wool*
*Paste and brush*
*Crayons or pencils*

1. Draw the outline of a boy or girl on a sheet of paper.
2. Help the child to 'dress' the doll using the scraps of fabric, filling in the outline of dress and socks or trousers and shirt.
3. When the doll's patchwork outfit is complete, use the wool to give it a fashionable hairdo.
4. Fill-in facial features using crayons or pencils.

☆ From 'jumble clothes' cut out a small zip, press-stud fastener, button and buttonhole and hook and eye. Keep the fasteners attached to the strips of fabric. Stick or staple the various fasteners on to a sheet of card and encourage child to practise fastening and unfastening.

# CRAFTWORK

Quite a bit of grown-up help is required with these activities — a friend got so involved with one project, she actually sent the children away in case they 'spoilt' it!

If you haven't room to store the ironing board — a 'craft cupboard' will sound a bit romantic! But to buy basic craft materials is ridiculously expensive especially when you realize that much useful material passes through your hands as rubbish every day.

## MATERIALS TO SAVE

Greetings cards

Rinsed clean paper plates

Cardboard rolls from toilet paper, kitchen tissue, foil and cling film

Ice cream cartons

Bottle tops

Straws

Card

Tissue paper

Margarine tubs and lids

Plastic meat and vegetable trays

Shells

Attractive stones and pebbles

Cotton wool

Scraps of fabric and wool

Wrapping paper

## SUNFLOWER MEASURING CHART

*A length of plain paper,
    approximately 100 × 20 cm
    (3 ft × 8 in)
1 small paper plate
Yellow paint
Scraps of green paper
Blu-Tack
Crayons or felt-tip pens
A few sunflower seeds (optional)
Metre rule
Paste and brush*

1. Draw a thick, green 'stem' down the centre of the paper. Measure and mark-off the stem in centimetres from 1 to 100 cm ( ½ in to 3 ft).

2. Blu-Tack the chart on to the child's bedroom wall at the correct height.

3. Paint the top side of the plate yellow. When dry, make small snips all the way around the edge to resemble petals.

4. In the centre of the flower plate, draw a 'smiley' face. On the cheeks, stick a few sunflower seeds.

5. Cut six or more leaf shapes from the green paper. Stick two to the bottom of the wall chart.

6. Measure child against chart and using Blu-Tack, stick the sunflower into position to indicate height.

7. As the child grows and the flower gets moved up the chart record each stage with a leaf giving date and age.

## PEBBLE PET PAPERWEIGHT

*A medium-sized pebble or stone,
    scrubbed
Paints or felt-tip pens
Varnish
Brush*

1. Simply paint or draw faces on the pebbles or stones. Discuss the shape and colour of the pebble. See if it resembles any particular animal and paint it

accordingly. Young children will probably feel more confident decorating with simple patterns: allow one colour to dry before applying another.

2. When dry, give the pebble pet a coat of varnish to protect it and give a sheen.

## SIMPLE WEAVE TABLEMATS

☆ Weaving illustrates the meaning of the words 'under', 'over' and 'through'.

*Stiff coloured or patterned card (cereal and washing powder packets are ideal)*
*Scissors*
*Ruler*
*Stape gun and staples*

1. Cut two pieces of card 15 cm (6 in) square.

2. Cut squares into 2 cm (¾ in) wide strips, leaving strips of the second square attached at the top 'fringe-like'. (This keeps the vertical strips in place and makes 'weaving' the horizontal ones easier.)

3. Taking one strip at a time, show the child how to weave it under and over the vertical strips. Start the first strip under and over, the second over and under, and so on.

4. When all the strips are used, hold the 'mat' in position while the child secures each corner with a staple.

5. The mat can be left as it is or finished with a border of sticky tape.

It is often worth giving a child some basic materials and letting his or her imagination run riot. Given a cardboard tube, most children will peer through it, using it as a periscope, or turn it into a trumpet!

☆ Try using plain card in contrasting colours or painting your own pattern on plain card. It's fascinating to see how the pattern looks when cut and woven.

## FUN BOOKMARKS

☆ When making these as gifts, look out for appropriate pictures to use as decorations: a flower for a gardener; a ball of knitting wool for a knitter; and so on.

*Greetings cards with bright, bold illustrations*
*Stiff, plain card (the backs of the greetings cards are fine)*
*Double-sided sticky pads*
*Scissors*

1. Help the child to cut around the head of the greetings card animal or 'character'. (Draw a simple outline as a guide for young children.)
2. Show child how to measure and cut a strip of stiff card, 3 cm × 15 cm (1¼ in × 6 in) long.
3. Using the sticky pad, stick the 'cut out' to the top of the card. The pad needs to be near the top of the 'cut out' to allow it to 'hook' over the page.

## SHEEP MOBILES

*Small paper plate*
*Stiff white card*
*Cotton wool*
*Paste and brush*
*Pipe cleaners*
*Thread*
*Crayons or felt-tip pens*

1. Paint the inside of the plate pale blue to resemble the sky.
2. Help the child to draw and cut out five sheep (just heads and bodies) from stiff card. Make a template for the child to draw around. Simply draw a large oval for the body and a small one for the head. Sheep should be about 10 cm (4 in) long.

3. Cut pipe cleaners into twenty 2 cm (¾ in) lengths and stick four under each sheep, two each side, to resemble legs.

4. Paste cotton wool coats to both sides of each sheep. Using crayons or felt-tip pens, draw eyes and noses.

5. Cut five pieces of thread, 5 × 15 cm (2 in × 6 in) in length. Attach one end of each thread to the back of a sheep. Thread the other end evenly around the edge of the plate and tie to secure.

6. Hang the mobile from the ceiling by another length of thread.

## ROCKET SKITTLES

*Six cardboard tubes from toilet rolls*
*Paint*
*Scissors*
*Stiff card*
*Lightweight ball*

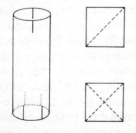

1. Make 2 cm (¾ in) cuts into each end of the cardboard tubes, two either side at the top, four evenly spaced around the bottom.

2. Using the stiff card, cut out three pieces, each 6 cm (2½ in) square. Cut squares diagonally to make six triangles (the rocket heads). Slot one into the top of each tube.

3. Make twelve more triangles by cutting six 8 cm (3¼ in) squares of stiff card diagonally. Cut six triangles from the point to the centre of the triangle.

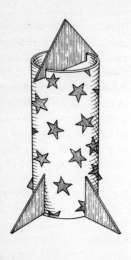

Cut the remaining six from the centre of the base up to the middle of the triangle.

4. Slot a triangle with a slit in the bottom over one with a slit in the top (six rocket bases).

5. Fit the base into the slits in the bottom of each tube.

6. Paint or decorate the skittle rockets and take it in turns to try and knock over the rockets with a ball.

7. Discuss the various shapes being cut out and number the skittles to see who can get the highest score.

## TRINKET BOXES

*Margarine or cream cheese tubs and salad containers with lids*
*Scraps of wrapping paper and magazine pictures*
*Paste and brush*
*Ribbons, tinsel, shells*
*Varnish (optional)*

1. Cut the wrapping paper or magazine into small squares, roughly 2.5 cm (1 in) square.

2. Use these paper squares to cover the slides of the tub or container. Work on small areas at a time, pasting the tub and overlapping the paper to ensure there are no gaps.

3. Paste and cover the tub or container lid in exactly the same way. (Leave the outside rims clear, so that these make a neat edging.)

4. When the tub is dry, it can be varnished.

5. Trim and decorate with small bows, ribbons, tinsel, or shells.

## WEATHER CHART

A sheet of stiff card, approximately 40 cm (16 in) square

Old colour magazines and catalogues

Paste and brush

Scissors

Butterfly clip

A strip of plastic or stiff card, approximately 2 cm × 8 cm (¾ in × 3¼ in)

1. Draw a line down the middle and across the middle of the card to divide it into quarters.
2. Look through the magazines and catalogues, cutting out any pictures that illustrate sun, wind, rain and snow (clothes, scenes and games).
3. Help the child label the four sections – sunny, windy, raining and snowing.
4. Stick the pictures in the appropriate corners.
5. Make a hole and insert a butterfly clip through one end of the 'indicator' and the centre of the chart and secure.
6. Turn the indicator each day to show what the weather is.

> Collar stiffeners and plant labels make good 'indicators' for home-made charts.

☆ Similar charts can be made to show seasons and time of day. Making and using the charts provide lots of opportunity to talk about weather, and how the seasons change.

## PASTA AND DRINKING STRAW JEWELLERY

This sort of jewellery sells for a 'mint' in the boutiques – and this is original!

A selection of coloured straws and pasta (tubes, stars, shapes with a hole through the centre)

Shirring elastic

Large blunt sewing needle

Empty egg carton

Scissors

1. Cut the straws into varying lengths up to 2 cm (¾ in).
2. Arrange the various pasta shapes and straws in the egg cups of the egg carton.
3. Cut lengths of elastic, 30 cm (12 in) for a necklace, 10 cm

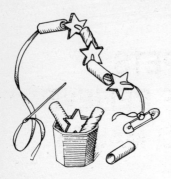

(4 in) for a bracelet. Tie one end of the elastic to a safety pin, this prevents the 'beads' falling off.

4. Thread the other end through the needle.

5. Help the child to select and thread the 'beads' on to the elastic until it is full.

6. Untie or snip the elastic from safety pin, unthread from needle and tie the two ends together.

## STAINED GLASS PICTURES

*Two sheets of fairly stiff black paper approximately 25 cm (10 in) square*

*A sheet of tissue paper the same size as above*

*Paste and brush*

*Scissors*

*Blu-Tack*

1. With two sheets together, fold the black paper in half and along the folded edge cut out a shape (a simple shape for young children, half a house or a butterfly wing for older children). When the paper is unfolded it discloses a full butterfly, a complete house.

2. Open out the paper and spread a little paste around the edges of one side of both sheets.

3. Lay the tissue between the pasted sides of the black paper and smooth down – a tissue sandwich!

4. Blu-Tack the stained glass picture to a window or hang it where the sun will shine though.

5. Don't take over. Children can tackle most of these activities with a little 'help'.

# PUPPETS AND MAKE BELIEVE HATS AND MASKS

From simple faces drawn on hands or even fingers to elaborate string-controlled models, children adore puppets. They get a lot of satisfaction from making and operating their own and this can be done quite easily.

The easiest puppets are made by simply drawing a face on a plain paper bag and using it as a glove puppet. Alternatively use an old sock or spare piece of material sewn in a square. Do encourage children to put on puppet shows and plays. The puppet 'theatre' is another opportunity to use newly acquired painting and craftwork skills – expanding imagination as well as numerous individual skills. Clap at everything: better to be safe than thought of as unappreciative!

## MATERIALS TO SAVE

| | |
|---|---|
| Socks | Sticks |
| Ties | Straws |
| Card | Scraps of paper |
| Yoghurt/margarine | and fabric |
| tubs | Buttons and trimmings |

## FLOWER POT PEOPLE

*Yoghurt pot*
*A straw or short stick*
*Stiff card*
*A pipe cleaner coloured green or*
*  a scrap of green crêpe paper*
*Sticky tape*
*Crayons or felt-tip pens*

1. Cut a circle from stiff card, draw around an egg cup as a guide.
2. Colour the circle a pretty colour, snip around the edge to make petals and using crayons or felt-tip pens give the 'flower' a smiley face.
3. Attach flower to end of straw with sticky tape.
4. Cut pipe cleaner in half, twist one half around straw to resemble leaves (a strip of paper can be tied around straw).
5. Help by puncturing a small hole (just big enough for the straw to pass through) in the base of the yoghurt pot.
6. Poke the bottom of the straw into the pot and through the hole and by pushing it up and pulling it down make the flower appear and disappear.

## TEDDY BEAR RING PUPPETS

*Stiff card*
*Cardboard tube from toilet roll*
*Paste and brush or stapler and*
*  staples*
*Scissors*
*Crayons or felt-tip pens*

1. Help the child to draw and cut out a teddy bear shape about 13 cm (5 in) tall. (Make a template and show the child how to draw around it.)
2. Using crayons or felt-tip pens, colour and draw eyes and other features.
3. Slice a ring, approximately

2.5 cm (1 in) deep, from the tube – a job for an adult.
4. Staple or stick ring to back of teddy to give a handle.
5. Holding on to the ring, make teddy dance and jig.

☆ Sandwich a drinking straw between two cut-out fish made from hand prints and make him swim in and out. Stick puppets are really simple to make. Just tape a short stick or straw to the back of a card doll, scarecrow, witch, or animal and you have a puppet.

You can make all sorts of ring puppets, drawing your own or cutting them from magazines and comics and sticking them on to stiff card.

Young children do not have the control to cut around intricate shapes, but don't take over the cutting out. Frame the shape to be cut out in a simple square and encourage the child to use that as the cutting line.

---

*Don't throw away 'odd' or outgrown socks. Sew or stick two buttons for eyes and two triangles of felt for ears on the sole of the sock; and, with a triangle of felt on the toe for a nose you have a puppy glove puppet.*

---

## INCEY WINCEY SPIDER

*Egg box (not the plastic variety)*
*Four pipe cleaners cut in half*
*Black paint*
*Thin elastic*
*Scraps of black and white paper*

1. Help the child to cut out one egg 'cup' for each spider and paint it black.
2. Make eight small holes around the edge of the cup (pre-school children are too young to 'puncture' holes but do get them to count the correct number).

*Do encourage children to recite relevant nursery rhymes and songs. If they attend a play group they will probably know more than you can remember. If you have both forgotten don't 'lose face', sneak a look at the 'Rhymes and Songs' section.*

3. Poke the eight pipe cleaner legs through the holes bending them inside the cup to hold fast. Bend each pipe cleaner into a 'Z' shape to resemble spider's legs.
4. Stick two circles of white paper on the front of the cup and two smaller circles of black paper on top for Incey's beady eyes.
5. Finally, thread a length of elastic through the top of the cup for Incey to climb (bounce) up and down.

## SAMMY SPIRAL SNAKE

*A circle of stiff card approximately 18 cm (7 in) in diameter (use a tea plate as a guide)*
*Scissors*
*A short length of thread*

1. Beginning at the outside edge draw a line making a pattern of ever decreasing circles to the middle of the circle. Keep the circles approximately 3 cm (1¼ in) apart.
2. Cut along the line taking care not to cut across the circles. Help by holding the circle and gradually turning it as the child cuts.
3. Tie a short length of thread to the centre (tail) of the circle. Draw two eyes and a long red tongue on the other (head) end.
4. Pull up the thread to discover twirly, curly Sammy Spiral Snake.

## SAMMY SNAKE ALTERNATIVE

*An old tie or length of fabric around 40 cm (16 in) long and 6 cm (2½ in) wide, sewn to form a point at both ends*
*Two small circles of felt*
*One small rectangle of red or black fabric for the tongue*
*Glue or stapler and staples*
*String or thread*
*A stick or short garden cane about 25 cm (10 in) long*

1. If using a tie, cut it in half (a full-length tie is too long for a young child to control) and turn in and stick the cut edge to make a 'point' (the tail).
2. Stick or staple the two felt circles to the 'head' of the snake about 8 cm (3¼ in) from the end. Cut a 'V' shape from one end of the rectangle and stick or staple it under the point or 'mouth' of the snake to resemble a forked tongue.
3. Attach two threads, about 20 cm (8 in) long, one just behind the eyes, the other to the middle of the snake.
4. Tie the two threads, one to either end of the stick. Hold the stick in the middle and make Sammy Snake slither along the ground.

## TUBE TOWN FOLK

*Cardboard rolls from toilet rolls or foil*
*Scraps of fabric, wool and cotton wool*
*Paste and brush*
*Trimmings*
*Crayons or felt-tip pens*

1. Cover the bottom two-thirds of the tube with fabric or paper. Choose something appropriate: velvet or glossy paper for a king or queen, a pretty floral print for mum, gingham for the 'tube twins' and so on.
2. Using crayons or felt-tip pens, draw a face on the uncovered tube.

3. For hair, stick on strands of wool or cotton wool. Top with a little triangle of material headscarf, a paper crown, a paper tiara or pirate's hat.

4. Trim with buttons, bows, cotton wool beards, sticky tape ties, and any other suitable accessories.

## SIMPLE HATS

**Children love playing with hats. Paper ones are simple to make and fun to wear.**

*Bands of stiff paper long enough to fit around the child's head, plus overlap to stick or staple*
*Paste and brush*
*Stapler and staples*
*Crayons or felt-tip pens*
*Trimmings – beads, sequins, scraps of fabric and wrapping paper.*

★ *KING OR QUEEN'S CROWN*

Help the child to cut a 'crocodile tooth' edge along the top of the band. Decorate with beads and glittery paper. Staple or stick the ends of the band to form a crown.

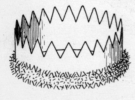 

★ *FAIRY*

Cut a band approximately 3 cm (1¼ in) deep. Decorate it with tinsel and glitter. Cut a star shape from stiff paper, brush with paste and glitter and fasten it to the front of the band. Secure at the back.

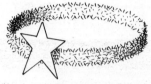

★ *PIRATE*

Use black card. Measure the band, cut in half. Shape the top of both halves into a bridge shape. Staple sides of bands together and crayon, chalk or felt tip a skull and crossbones on the front.

★ *INDIAN*

Decorate band with brightly coloured zig-zag patterns. Cut long feather shapes from coloured card and staple to band. Secure at back.

## ★ CLOWNS AND WIZARDS

Cut a circle of stiff paper using a tea plate as a guide. Make one cut from the circumference to the middle and overlap the edges to make a cone shape. Attach a strap of elastic to either side of the hat. Use black paper and decorate with foil moons and stars for the wizard. Use bright paper card and decorate with cut out flowers on drinking straw 'stems' for the clown.

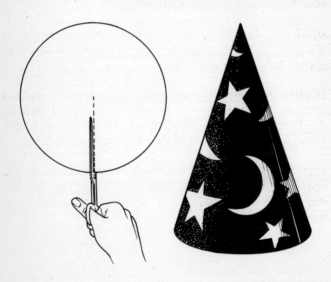

Dressing-up boxes do not have to be full of 'couture' dressing-up outfits. Outgrown mini-slips make ideal wedding dresses, any waistcoat will do for 'Billy the Kid'. A threadbare blue towel will probably see service as a nurse's cape and superman's cape. One little boy spent one happy afternoon wearing a Sixties sequinned 'boob tube' around his head. I've no idea who he was meant to be!

## ANIMAL MASKS

*Bands of stiff paper long enough*
*to fit around the child's head*
*and fasten*
*Scissors*
*Stapler and staples*
*Crayons*

★ **BEAR** Use brown paper. Cut around two semi-circles either side of the centre of the headband to resemble ears. Secure band at back.

★ **DUCK** Use yellow paper. Cut band with a deep V in the centre. Staple together the two arms of the V to give a beak. Secure at back.

★ **DONKEY** Use grey paper. Cut two feather shapes around 20 cm (8 in) long from stiff card. Pinching the bottom end of each 'feather', staple them to the band to resemble 'donkey's ears'. Secure at back.

☆ Play binoculars and goggles can be made by taping together two cardboard inner tubes and by cutting the bottoms out of a pair of egg box cups and threading elastic through the sides.

# GAMES

## TABLE GAMES

The simplest game to make is a jigsaw. Help your child to choose a picture from a magazine and paste it on to some stiff card. When dry, divide and cut into nine or more pieces. Store the pieces in an envelope. When you open this up later, you will have your own home-made jigsaw.

Playing simple card and counter dice games helps develop recognition and co-ordination skills. They are quite inexpensive to buy and they can also be made very easily.

## MATERIALS TO SAVE

| | |
|---|---|
| Magazines | Stiff card |
| Greetings cards | Corks |
| Magnets | Sponge |
| Paper clips | |

### MATCH THE LEGS TO THE BODY

*Six or more magazine pictures of animals (the animals must be standing)*

1. Stick the animal pictures on separate pieces of card.
2. When dry, cut each picture in

*Stiff card*
*Paste and brush*
*Scissors*

two separating the bodies from the legs.

3. Shuffle the picture halves around on the table and ask the child to match the correct legs to the bodies. When this gets too simple turn the pictures face down and take it in turns to see who can remember where the various halves are. If you select two corresponding halves you keep them.

☆ Children enjoy playing 'Guess what's in the Bag'. Place a familiar object – a small doll, spoon, shoe, or saucepan lid in the bag. Allow the child to feel and squeeze for a few seconds before telling you what's in the bag! When the child gets more competent put two or more items in the bag.

## FISHING GAME

*Sheet of stiff card, approximately 60 cm (24 in) wide and 20 cm (8 in) deep*
*Paper clips*
*Small magnets (you can buy these in packs of six quite cheaply from toy shops)*
*Short sticks*
*String*
*Paste and brush or stapler and staples*
*Stiff card for fish*

1. Make the fish tank by pasting or stapling the ends of the stiff card together to make a tube.

2. Draw, colour and cut out six small fish shapes around 5 cm (2 in) long.

3. Clip a paper clip to the head of each fish (it is the metal paper clips that will be attracted by the magnet).

4. Taking a stick for each player tie a length of string approximately 25 cm (10 in) long to one end. Tie a magnet to the other end of the string. The

> At Christmas, swop the tank for a chimney pot and 'fish' for Santa and his parcels!

game is to 'hook' out as many fish as possible. Add a few old can and boot shapes for fun, and, for older children, number the fish to see who can get the highest score.

> Ask one child to draw a head on the top of a strip of paper. Fold this behind, out of sight and get another child to draw the body. Fold this drawing out of sight and get a third child to draw the legs – unfold the paper to reveal a Bitzer (bits of this and bits of that).

## PICTURE SETS

*Pictures of animals, cars and flowers. They should be around 12 cm (4¾ in) square and you will need one picture per player*
*Stiff card*
*Paste and brush*
*Scissors*
*Crayon or felt-tip pens*
*Dice*

1. Help the child or children to stick the pictures on to stiff card. When dry, cut each picture into six even-sized pieces.
2. Number the pieces of each picture from one to six. Label the pieces with both a number and dots. 5 ∴ for example.
3. Take it in turns to throw the dice and 'win' the piece of picture with the same number as thrown. The winner completes the picture jigsaw first.

☆ Cover a dice with sticky paper in different colours and play picture sets, replacing numbers with colours to help develop familiarity with colours.

## MEMORY GAME

*Eight household items small enough to fit together on a tray*

1. Place the items on the tray. Discuss each item for a minute or so.

*A tray*
*A cloth to cover the tray*

Button, screw and coin collections can be graded and divided between the 'cups' in an egg box according to size or length.

2. Cover the tray and its contents with the cloth and see how many items the child can remember. Ask the child to study the items on the tray for a minute, then ask him or her to turn around while you removed one item. What is missing from the tray?

☆ Place an empty margarine tub on the table and ask the child to find six items that he thinks will fit into the tub. How accurate was the selection?

☆ Who can fit the most things into a matchbox?

## COLOUR SCRAPBOOKS

*Large sheets of stiff paper*
*Stapler and staples or paper*
  *punch and wool*
*Paste and brush*
*Old magazines and catalogues*
*Scissors*

1. Either staple or punch and tie three or four sheets of stiff paper together to make a book.
2. Help the child to label the front cover 'Colour Scrapbook' and to decorate it with pictures.
3. Allow one page for each colour. Write the colour at the top of the page and draw a paintpot or pencil in the appropriate colour beside it. (A grown-up will have to do the writing.)
4. Look through magazines and catalogues cutting out the best pictures. Sort out the pictures into colour groups and paste them into the scrapbook on the correct pages.

☆ Fill scrapbooks with all sorts of picture collections of animals, Royal Family, flowers and trees, etc., or with souvenirs from holidays and outings.

## SIMPLE TAPESTRY

*Greetings cards*
*A large blunt needle*
*A bradawl or pointed needle for making holes*
*Stiff card*
*Coloured wool*

> Dot-to-dot pictures are simple to create substituting a pencil for a needle. Just draw a simple picture with a broken outline and show child how to join it up with pencil lines.

1. Select a card with a bold picture on the front.
2. A grown-up is needed here to puncture holes around the outline of the picture at about 1 cm (½ in) intervals.
3. Help the child thread the needle with a piece of wool (about 35 cm (14 in) long). Tie a knot in the end to prevent wool being pulled straight through.
4. Show the child how to sew around the outline, poking the needle through the ready-made holes in a simple slip stitch.

☆ Draw the child's initial on a piece of stiff card, and puncture small holes in the outline for the child to sew.

## SINK OR FLOAT

Close supervision is needed when involved in the sink or float game. Turn away for a moment and you could find your best watch or the pet hamster in the 'deep'!

*A deep container, preferably glass*
*Water*
*Objects – corks, pebbles, bottle tops, spoons, sponges, and so on*

1. Fill the container two-thirds full with water.
2. Discuss each item, and try and guess whether it will sink or float. Place each item in the water and see who guessed correctly. Show the difference

between heavy and light objects. Demonstrate how the sponge becomes heavy as it soaks up the water.

---

*Allow the child to spoon a little salt into a cup of water and watch it dissolve. Remember the fable about the 'silly ass' who thought he was clever dissolving his loads of salt in the river until his master gave him a different load to carry – sponges!*

---

## ANYTIME, ANYWHERE GAMES

You don't always need props to play games. You can play 'I spy' type games when you are travelling, queuing, or shopping in the supermarket. I can't guarantee that children will always want to join in: seeing how far you can lean back while riding on the front of the trolley or selecting your own favourite biscuits from the shelves could well seem like more fun!

Things can be confusing even when the child becomes familiar with letters and sounds. In a recent game I was asked to find something beginning with 'ch'. Only to discover when I'd 'given up' that the answer I was looking for was supposed to be 'train'!!!

★ *I SPY*    When you begin to play I spy make the clues easy. 'I spy with my little eye something big and red – bus' 'I spy with my little eye something brown and with a buckle – shoe'

★ *TALLEST,*    A very simple observation game.
  *SHORTEST*    The idea is to find the tallest thing you can see, the shortest, the loudest, the fastest . . . .

★ *TEN QUESTIONS*   Ask the child to think of a favourite food, person or TV programme. You are allowed to ask just ten questions before you try and guess the answer. Take it in turns to try and guess.

★ *YES, NO*   Try to answer as many questions as you can without using the words 'yes' and 'no'. Children find this very difficult. Do suggest some alternative answers to them: 'I do not', 'I will', and so on.

★ *COUNTING GAMES*   When travelling in a car or train, see how many red cars or green houses you can count. See who can be the first to see a bridge, a cow, a sports car . . . .

★ *STORYTELLING*   Start telling a story, ask child what would happen next. Take it in turns to make up the story until someone thinks of a good ending.

★ *ONE MINUTE'S WORTH*   This is easier if you have a second hand on your watch. How many colours can you think of in one minute. How many animals, boys' names, girls' names, different forms of transport? If you are travelling, see how many 'GB' signs, aerials, lorries, or caravans you see in one minute.

★ *SIMON SAYS*   A real old favourite. You only

follow the instruction if it begins with 'Simon Says'. If Simon says 'stand up', you stand up, but if you are told simply to 'stand up' you stay still. Children like both to give and receive the orders.

☆ If it has been a bad day you could always try 'a minute's silence'. See if the children can keep absolutely quiet for one whole minute – tell yourself you are playing the game to show them how long a minute lasts!

# COOKING

Cooking must be one of the most popular activities. It is a marvellous way to learn about the way things grow, what we need to stay healthy and about hygiene. It encourages children to follow instructions, introduces weighing, measuring, mixing, and pouring, and there's usually something edible to show at the end!

Kitchen activities should be supervised at all times both from the safety angle and because as soon as you turn your back a packet of salt will go in the burgers, the cake mix will end up on the floor or, as happened recently, a tub of mint was stirred into a couple of tablespoons of potato salad.

Don't ignore the packet mixes. Bread mixes are convenient, easy to use and offer the chance to try things that might otherwise be too complicated for children to tackle. Besides, children aren't as 'snobbish' about home cooking as the grown-ups!

Do get children into the habit of washing their hands before tackling any food preparation. Show young children how to wash properly. Most believe that 'flashing' one hand under a cold running tap is sufficient.

Don't present children with ingredients ready weighed, eggs beaten and cake tins greased. They learn a lot and enjoy doing that tasks that we do without thinking, including the washing-up and clearing away at the end of the cooking session.

Bread and butter must be the simplest 'dish' to prepare but it still requires the skills of spreading and cutting. Use an easy-spreading margarine or butter substitute. It will 'go' further.

## DOUBLE DECKER SANDWICHES

*2 slices of brown bread*
*1 slice white bread*
*Cream cheese*

1. Cut crusts of all three slices of bread.
2. Spread one slice of brown bread and one slice of white bread with cream cheese.
3. Top the cheese spread brown slice with the white slice and cover with the second brown slice.
4. Cut the Double Decker into fingers.

## EASY BAP PIZZAS

*One bread bap*
*Two tablespoons of tomato ketchup or a small tin of chopped tomatoes*
*Two slices of cheese or 50 g (2 oz) grated cheese (grate from a large chunk of cheese so that little fingers are not close to the cutting edge)*
*Salt and pepper*

*(To make two pizzas)*

1. Split the bap in half and lay the two sides flat.
2. Spread each bap with either a tablespoon of ketchup or chopped tomatoes.
3. Top each bap with a slice or 25 g (1 oz) of cheese and season with salt and pepper.
4. Pop Pizza Baps under the grill until the cheese has melted. (Grilling is best left to a grown-up.)

## POTATO SALAD

*225 g ( ½ lb) potatoes, boiled*
*Two tablespoons salad cream or mayonnaise*

1. Help the child to chop potatoes into small chunks (use a chopping board).

Salt and pepper
A few leaves of mint, chopped.
   (Do let the children smell this
   herb and explain that herbs
   make food taste better and can
   be used to cure the sick)

2. Put the potatoes, salad cream or mayonnaise, salt and pepper and a 'pinch' of mint into a bowl.
3. Mix all the ingredients together with a spoon. Cover and chill in the fridge.

☆ Do explain where potatoes come from (you may have a hard time convincing them it isn't the supermarket!). If you don't know an obliging gardener, let a potato go to seed to demonstrate how they grow. Most children are amazed to hear that mash, waffles, chips and most of all, crisps are all made from potato.

---

Rinse out an empty egg shell, stuff it with damp cotton wool. Using felt-tip pens, draw a face on the front of the shell and 'sit' it in an egg cup. Sprinkle a few mustard and cress seeds on top of the cotton wool and watch the head of mustard and cress hair grow.

---

## BEEFBURGERS

For each burger:
50 g (2 oz) mince
One teaspoon chopped onion
One teaspoon beaten egg
Salt and pepper
A little flour

Explain that the **ingredients** are the different types of food we use when cooking and that **utensils** are the tools that we need to cook.

1. Help the child to weigh the mince. Place it in a bowl with onion, egg, salt and pepper.
2. Mix ingredients together with a fork.
3. Turn the mixture out on to a lightly floured board and pat into a flattish cake.
4. Pop the burger on to a plate, cover and chill for 30 minutes before passing over to an adult to grill or fry.

☆ When weighing foods, take it in turns – one spooning out while the other checks the scales, then swapping jobs. This teaches children what measuring actually is and the beginnings of how much things actually weigh.

---

*Slice the top off a fresh carrot, place it in a saucer of water, leave it on the window sill and wait for it to sprout. You can do this with most root vegetables.*

---

## ICED BISCUITS

Spread plain biscuits with a little glacé icing made from a couple of tablespoons of icing sugar and a few drops of hot water and they can be decorated in a dozen ways. The icing should be the consistency of a thin paste: soft enough to spread but not so watery that it runs off the biscuit. Colour it with a little food colouring if wanted.

★ *TRAFFIC LIGHTS* Spread icing on Rich Tea Fingers and decorate with 'traffic lights' (red, green and amber Smarties).

★ *HAPPY FACES* Ice Digestive or round Rich Tea biscuits and decorate with Dolly Mixture faces and vermicelli hair.

★ *NAME BISCUITS* If serving iced biscuits at parties, ice Rich Tea Fingers or digestive biscuits with glacé icing then pipe the names or the initials of the party guests in contrasting icing.

## RICE CRISPY CAKES

*One block of cooking chocolate (milk chocolate, as plain tends to be sickly and an awful lot of 'finger licking' usually goes on)*

*One tablespoon margarine or butter*

*Rice Krispies*

1. Melting chocolate is best left to an adult. Break chocolate into pieces in a glass bowl. Stand the bowl into another containing hot water and leave until the chocolate is 'runny'. Stir until smooth.
2. Add margarine or butter. (This prevents the chocolate hardening.)
3. Stir in Rice Krispies until all the chocolate is used up. Make sure the Krispies are all coated or the cakes will fall apart.
4. Drop spoonfuls of the mixture into paper cake cases ('petit four' cases are ideal for the very young).
5. Leave to set.

☆ Cornflakes can be substituted for Rice Krispies.

☆ The Rice Crispy mixture can be pressed into an oiled square tin and when set, cut into fingers.

## SMARTIE CAKES

*50 g (2 oz) self-raising flour*
*50 g (2 oz) caster sugar*
*50 g (2 oz) soft margarine*

1. Heat oven to 180°C, Gas Mark 4.
2. Arrange twelve paper cake cases (or twenty-four 'petit four' cases)

*Pinch of baking powder*
*One egg, lightly beaten*
*50 g (2 oz) icing sugar*
*A little hot water*
*Smarties*

---

Children can make
their own Chocolate
Milk by stirring two to
three teaspoons of
drinking chocolate
into one-third of a
pint of milk and
topping with a scoop
of vanilla ice cream
and a chocolate
flake.

---

in one or two bun tins.

3. Put flour, margarine, sugar, egg and baking powder in a bowl and mix by hand or a free-standing electric mixer until all ingredients are thoroughly blended. (Young children should not use hand mixers.)

4. Using spoon and finger, divide the mixture between the cases (about two-thirds full).

5. Bake for around ten to twelve minutes ('petit four' cases), twelve to fifteen minutes (cake cases). Cool on a wire tray.

6. Blend icing sugar with a little hot water to make a thinnish paste. Put half to one teaspoon of icing on top of each cake and top with a Smartie.

## SCONES

*225 g (8 oz) self-raising flour*
*Pinch of salt*
*50 g (2 oz) margarine*
*Two tablespoons caster sugar*
*150 ml (¼ pint) milk*

---

Test an egg for
freshness – pop it in
a bowl of water. It
will float if fresh, sink
if bad!

---

1. Heat oven to 230°C, Gas Mark 8.
2. Grease a baking sheet.
3. Mix together flour and salt.
4. Show the child how to rub fat into flour using fingertips. Stir in sugar.
5. Pour in milk gradually, mixing with a round-bladed knife.
6. Tip dough on to floured board and knead until smooth.
7. Roll the dough out to a thick-ness of about 1 cm (½ in) and using a 5 cm (2 in) pastry

cutter, cut out scones (if cutter gets sticky, dip in flour). Mixture makes approximately twelve scones.

8. Place scones on baking tray and bake for around ten minutes until golden coloured. Leave on a wire tray to cool.

## SCONE BUTTER

*Full cream milk*
*Plastic tumbler*

1. Half fill a plastic tumbler (it must have an airtight lid) with full cream milk or 'top of the milk'.
2. Plop a clean marble into the tumbler, fit the lid on and shake and shake. After about fifteen minutes, small dots of butter will form.
3. Strain off the liquid and pat the butter dry – you won't be selling off the surplus but it's fun to make. The milk should be room temperature.

## BIRDCAKE – SOMETHING FOR THE BIRDS

*A yoghurt, margarine or cream*
  *cheese pot*
*A length of string, around 20 cm*
  *(8 in) long*
*100 g (4 oz) lard, melted*
*Breadcrumbs, cake and biscuit*
  *crumbs*
*Finely chopped bacon rind,*
  *chopped fruit, dried fruit, nuts*

1. Thread the string through the bottom of the pot, tie a knot to prevent it coming straight through. (It should look like a bell at this point.)
2. In a bowl, mix all the dry ingredients before pouring in the melted lard.
3. When all the ingredients are

well coated with lard, turn the pot the right way round and fill. Press the mixture firmly down in the pot. Leave to set before hanging from a tree or shed well away from the cat. Then sit back and spend an afternoon birdwatching. The pot can be refilled when empty.

# GIFT AND CRAFT IDEAS FOR SPECIAL OCCASIONS

Each year is highlighted by Special Occasions: New Year, Easter, Guy Fawkes Night and Christmas as well as lesser celebrated dates including Mothering Sunday and Halloween.

Children love making gifts and decorations to celebrate these events. Here are just a handful of ideas which will hopefully, give the inspiration for lots more.

Most of the following craft ideas require a considerable amount of adult supervision and help but remember — the results don't have to be perfect.

## NEW YEAR

### 'CLEVER COLIN/CONNIE CLOTHES COLLECTOR'

This dirty washing sack should help with the New Year's Resolution to keep bedrooms tidy.

*1 plain pillow case*
*1 straight coat hanger*
*Fabric pens or paints*
*Some plain paper for practising on*

1. Practise drawing a bright, portrait big enough to cover the front of the pillow case.
2. Place pillow case on a table, opening at the top, back facing.

When child is confident, help copy the portrait on to the back of the pillow case using fabric crayons or paints.

3. Slide the coat hanger under the flap of the pillow case and make a small snip in the crease just big enough to slip the coat hanger hook through (the hole really should be oversewn to prevent fraying but if that isn't part of your New Year's Resolution – forget it!).

4. Hang 'Clever Colin/Connie' over the end of the bed ready to collect dirty clothes.

## MOTHERING SUNDAY

Here are a couple of gift ideas for Mothering Sunday that 'Daddy' will have to lend a hand with!

### VASE OF TULIPS

*Inner tube from toilet roll*
*Piece of pretty wrapping paper, 14 cm × 16 cm (5½ × 6½ in)*
*3 'egg cups' cut from an egg carton (not the plastic variety)*
*3 straws or pipe cleaners*
*Small amount of plasticine or play dough*
*A piece of fairly stiff green*

1. Trim top of 'egg cups' to resemble tulip petals and paint red inside and out.
2. Make four 1.5 cm (⅝ in) cuts evenly around one end of the tube, fold in and fasten with sticky tape to form the base of the 'vase'.
3. Cover tube with wrapping paper tucking excess inside tube to give a neat edge.

paper approximately 15 cm
  × 6 cm (6 in × 2½ in)
Red paint
Sticky tape

4. Press small knob of plasticine into base of vase – this makes it more stable and holds fast the 'stems'.

5. Make a small hole in the base of each egg cup (this is a job for a grown up) and push the end of a straw or pipe cleaner through each hole. Cap each end with a tiny ball of plasticine.

6. Cut green paper into six leaves approximately 15 cm × 1 cm (6 in × ½ in). Tape the ends of two leaves to each stem and gently arrange 'tulips' in vase, pushing the bottoms of the 'stems' into the plasticine.

## MOTHERING SUNDAY KEEPSAKE HANDPRINT CARD

A piece of stiff card, 30 cm
  × 20 cm (12 in × 8 in)
Powder paint mixed fairly
  thickly with paste or starch
A shallow tray lined with a thin
  layer of sponge or foam

1. Fold the card in half to make a card 15 cm × 20 cm (6 in × 8 in). The fold should be at the top.

2. Pour a little paint on to the sponge or foam and allow it to soak in.

3. Help child to press first one hand then the other on to the paint pad and front of the card.

4. Leave the handprints to dry before writing the following verse inside:-

   'For you, a handprint not to wipe away

But to keep and remind you
of this special day!'

5. Help child to sign card by
writing it faintly so child can
write over it, or by outlining
name in dots and asking child
to join them.

☆ Have a bowl of soapy water and some spare paper
handy or you could find yourself spending the rest
of Mothering Sunday clearing up handprints you
aren't quite so happy keeping!

## EASTER

### MARBLE EGGS

*Paper*
*Oil paint (artists oils or
left-overs from the last
decorating job)*
*Paint thinner – do keep this
well away from the children!*
*Water*
*A shallow tray (paint pan trays
and old baking trays are ideal)*

*Keep a bottle of paint
remover handy but
out of the reach of
the children to deal
with splashes and
spills.*

1. Cut egg shapes out of the paper
– older children can do this if
given a cutting guide line.
2. Half fill tray with water.
3. Thin down oil paint slightly and
gently swirl a few tablespoonfuls
into the water. The oil and
water will not mix but give an
interesting marble effect.
4. Lay each 'paper egg' on top of
the water and gently lift them
off allowing excess paint and
water to drip back into tray.
5. Swirl paint around each time
before laying the next paper
egg down.

☆ Decorate the front of home-made Easter cards with
'marbled eggs'.

## EASTER CHICK PICTURES

*Washed and crushed egg shells*
*Stiff paper*
*Yellow cotton wool balls*
*Tiny scraps of black and*
*    orange felt*
*Glue*
*Glue spreader*

1. Using plain pastry cutter as a template, help child draw the bottom half of an egg with a zig zag 'cracked' top.
2. Cover the half egg shape with a thin coating of glue and fill in with a mosaic of crushed egg shell.
3. Dab a little glue on the back of two cotton wool balls for the body and head of the chick and sit them on the top of the egg shell.
4. Finish off the picture by giving little Easter chick two tiny black felt circles for eyes and a tri-angular orange felt beak.

## EASTER NEST CAKES

*Block of Milk Chocolate*
*1 tablespoon margarine*
*    or butter*
*2 or 3 shredded wheat, crumbled*
*12 chocolate mini eggs*
*12 paper cake cases*

1. Melt chocolate using method given in Rice Crispy Cake recipe (page 58).
2. Add margarine or butter and stir well.
3. Stir shredded wheat into chocolate mixture and make sure it is thoroughly coated.
4. Drop spoonfuls of mixture into paper cases – if an adult holds spoonfuls of mixture above the cases, children can scoop it off into the case using their own spoon.

5. Make a small dent in the top of each cake, sit a chocolate egg in each 'nest'. Leave to set.

## EASTER BONNET CAKES

*Round Rich Tea Biscuits*
*Glacé icing made with icing*
*    sugar and water*
*Marshmallows*
*Sugar flowers, hundreds and*
*    thousands, scraps of ribbon*
*    etc. for decoration.*

1. Cover top of biscuits with glacé icing.
2. Place a marshmallow in the centre of the icing.
3. Decorate the 'bonnet' with sweets, flowers, ribbons etc.

# HALLOWEEN

## PUMPKIN FACE

*Stiff black card approximately,*
*    20 cm × 30 cm (8 in × 12 in)*
*Orange tissue paper*
*Glue*
*Glue spreader*
*Cord*
*Scraps of black paper*

1. Help child draw a large pumpkin shape on the stiff card.
2. Cut out the pumpkin shape. This is quite difficult and probably best left to a grown up – it is the surrounding frame that is to be used, not the pumpkin shape.
3. Lay the pumpkin shape on top of the orange tissue paper. Use it as a guide and leaving a border of around 1 cm (½ in) cut around the tissue paper.
4. Carefully run the glue spreader around the outline of the pumpkin on the 'frame'. Lay the tissue pumpkin over the frame

and press the edges down firmly.

5. Turn the picture over to the right side and give Pumpkin man a face, sticking on two black triangular eyes, a large triangular nose and a big, smiling semi circular mouth.

6. Make a small hole in the top of the 'frame', thread a length of cord through and hang in front of a window or light to see Pumpkin Face glow!

☆ Pumpkins aren't difficult to draw, they are simply circles with dents in the top!

☆ Lollipops wrapped in soft white tissue and decorated with ghostly features make good Ghostie-pops.

## GUY FAWKES NIGHT

### BONFIRE PICTURES

*Paper*
*Black paint, mixed*
  *fairly thinly*
*Wax crayons in bright colours*
*Paint brush*

1. Using the coloured crayons and pressing firmly draw a bright Bonfire Night picture on the paper.

2. Brush the paint very lightly over the surface of the paper.

3. The paint will not stick to the waxed surface so the crayoned pattern will appear to shine through a black night sky.

☆ The children love helping to make Catherine Wheel sandwiches. They like eating them as well when they have become bored with the fireworks and have left the adults to their ooooohing and aaaaahing!

## CATHERINE WHEEL SANDWICHES

*A thin sliced Loaf*
*Cream cheese*

1. Cut the crusts from the slices of bread.
2. Spread each slice thinly with cream cheese.
3. Roll each slice into a 'swiss roll' shape – this is easier if an adult starts the roll off.
4. Wrap in cling film or foil and chill for 30 minutes.
5. Unwrap and slice into thin 'Catherine Wheel' slices.

☆ Use brown bread if possible, it contrasts with the cheese and makes a more impressive Catherine Wheel.

## EVERLASTING SPARKLERS

*A sheet of stiff paper*
*A drinking straw or thin stick*
*Glue*
*Glue spreader*
*Glitter*

1. Help child to glue straw or stick on to paper – spread the glue on the paper not the straw.
2. Dab glue sparingly in a random pattern around the end of the straw.
3. Sprinkle glitter over the glue daubs to make an everlasting sparkler.
4. Shake paper over a tray to get rid of any loose glitter.
5. Experiment making different patterns, drawing glue initials etc. to make a variety of sparkler pictures.

☆ Here is a good opportunity to explain to young children about throwing 'used' sparklers away and not grabbing the hot end with a free hand!

## TUBE ROCKETS

*Inner tubes from toilet rolls*
*Red tissue paper*
*Long drinking straws or*
*   thin canes*
*Colouring crayons or paints*
*Sticky tape*

1. Colour the outside of the tubes with either crayons or paints. Make them bright and powerful looking.
2. Place one end of drinking straw along tube and secure top and bottom of tube with sticky tape.
3. Cut a rough circle of red tissue paper around 15 cm (6 in) in diameter. Tuck the red tissue in the base of the 'rocket' and secure with sticky tape. Leave enough paper showing to give the rocket a real 'blast off' look.

☆ These rockets cost a lot less than the real thing, make less noise, are less dangerous and there's an outside chance that they will last fractionally longer!

## CHRISTMAS

## POT POURRI CHRISTMAS CRACKERS

*Cardboard inner tubes from*
*   foil, kitchen roll, aluminium*
*   foil, toilet rolls etc.*
*Rectangles of pretty, thin*
*   fabric, approximately 15 cm*

1. Cut an 8 cm (3¼ in) length of inner tube – you will need a very sharp knife so this is best left to an adult as is the next step – piercing the tube all

× 23 cm (6 in × 9 in)
*Thin contrasting ribbon*
*A few tablespoons pot pourri*
*A needle for making holes
  in cardboard tube*
*Sticky tape*
*Glue*
*Glue spreader*

over using the needle. This will release more of the pot pourri perfume.

2. Seal one end of the tube with sticky tape. Stand tube on end and fill with pot pourri. Roll the tube of pot pourri up in the fabric. Where the fabric overlaps seal with glue.

3. Tie up the ends of the roll 'cracker' like and finish off with bows, gifts tags etc.

## A CHRISTMAS PUDDING PIN CUSHION

*Brown felt, approximately
  25 cm (12 in) square*
*Scraps of white, red and
  green felt*
*Kapok stuffing – small amount*
*Needle and strong thread*
*Glue*
*Glue spreader*

1. Using a tea plate as a guide, draw and cut out a circle of brown felt.

2. Draw a circle 1 cm (½ in) in from the outside edge and help child to sew running stitches around the inner circle. Secure the first stitch by overstitching two or three times.

3. Pull the last thread until the felt forms a little pouch. Leave enough of a gap to stuff the pouch with Kapok.

4. When the pouch is firmly filled, pull the thread until there is no gap and fasten off with a few firm stitches.

5. To decorate the 'pudding' cut a circle of white felt approximately 8 cm (3¼ in) in diameter (the children can do this, it

doesn't have to be accurate and certainly not perfect!)

6. Using the glue quite liberally, stick the felt 'cream' over the 'Christmas Pudding' – this looks good and hides the gathers and stitches.

7. All Christmas puddings should be topped with a sprig of holly. The holly for this pudding is made with two small diamonds of green felt and three tiny round red felt berries.

☆ If this is to be given as a present, it is a nice idea to fill it with coloured head pins.

## CHRISTMAS BELL

*Small yoghurt or cream pot*
*Aluminium foil*
*Cord*
*Needle*

1. Using a tea plate as a guide, help child draw and cut out a circle of aluminium foil.

2. Use the foil to cover the base and outside of the yoghurt pot tucking the excess inside the pot.

3. Cut a second circle of foil approximately the size of an egg cup.

4. Tie a knot two thirds of the way along the string. Make a small hole in the base of the pot and thread the long end of the string through. Turn the pot upside down and make a hanging loop in the top of the

string. Thread the other end of the string through the centre of the small circle of foil, tie a knot to secure it and scrunch the foil into a ball around the knot to make the bell hammer. Hang bell up.

## SNOWMAN SWEET HOLDER

*300 g (10 oz) cream carton with reusable lid*
*Cotton wool (the type that comes in a roll)*
*Glue*
*Glue spreader*
*Scraps of material, buttons etc. for trimming*

1. Liberally cover the outside and top of the carton with glue.
2. Unroll a little cotton wool and cut a circle big enough to cover the top of the carton and overlap slightly. Press down firmly.
3. Cut a length of cotton wool long enough to wrap around the outside of the carton and overlap slightly. Where the cotton wool overlaps stick down firmly with extra glue and smooth down with finger.
4. Using scraps of material, buttons etc. give Snowman two eyes, a nose, a mouth, a scarf and some buttons.
5. When dry, fill carton with sweets, soaps or other small gifts and snap on the reusable lid.

☆ You can make all sorts of containers in this way — cover carton with red paper to make a post box, cover with red fabric and trim with cotton wool for Father Christmas etc.

## CHRISTMAS TREE CARD

*Two sheets of stiff green card*

1. Place one sheet of card on top of the other.
2. Help child by making a bold Christmas tree template and showing him/her how to draw around it. Cut out the Christmas tree, cutting through both sheets of card at once.

   Fold the trees in half lengthways and then widthways to find the centre. Take one tree and cut from the base to the centre point. Take the second tree and cut from the top down to the centre point.
3. Slot the first tree over the second tree. The tree should now be freestanding. Help child write a Christmas message across the tree which can be folded flat for posting.

   The tree can be decorated with tiny silver balls and stars etc.

---

*If you run out of wrapping paper let the children decorate a sheet of plain white paper and you can end up looking inventive instead of forgetful. Gift tags can be made quickly by simply cutting shapes out of used gift cards – pinking shears give the best result!*

# BIRTHDAY PARTY IDEAS

If you have the time, birthday party invitations are easy and fun to make and you can carry the theme of the invitation through to the cake, prizes, etc. Here are a few simple ideas. If, however, organising the party is taking up all your spare minutes, pre-printed invitation pads are inexpensive and even easier!

## KITE INVITATIONS AND REPLY CARDS

*Some fairly stiff paper*
*Felt tip pens or crayons*
*Thin ribbon or cord*
*Self adhesive stars, shapes, etc.*

1. Draw and cut out as many 'kite' shapes as you require invitations. The easiest way to do this is to draw a cross approximately 15 cm (6 in) long × 10 cm (4 in) wide and join the ends of the cross to give a diamond shape longer at the bottom than the top.
2. Decorate two diagonal corners with bright shapes, etc.
3. Write relevant party details on plain corner, such as date, time, place, etc.
4. Using another colour stiff paper, cut out a bow shape approximately 10 cm (4 in) wide. (Make a template out of stiff card for both kite and bow and help child to draw around them).
5. Write, 'I can/cannot come to the party' on the bow.

6. Make a small hole in the bottom of the kite and in the middle of the reply bow. Thread a short length of ribbon or cord securing one end to the kite, the other to the 'tail'.

☆ Kite cakes are simple to make and can be decorated with chocolate buttons and sweets.

## HOT AIR BALLOON INVITATIONS AND REPLY CARDS

*Stiff coloured paper*
*Thin ribbon or cord*
*Felt tip pens or crayons*

1. Cut out as many balloon shapes as you may require invitations (approximately 10 cm (4 in) in diameter and an equal number of rectangles of about 6 cm (2½ in) × 4 cm (1½ in) deep. Make templates for child to draw around.
2. Write party details on balloon and decorate around edge with pens or crayons.
3. Write on rectangle 'baskets', 'I can/cannot come to the party'.
4. Make two holes either side of the base of the balloon. Thread the ends of two short lengths of ribbon through the holes in the balloon and tie a knot in each to secure. Make two holes in the top corners of the 'basket'. Thread the ends of the ribbon through the holes in the basket and tie a knot in each to secure.

☆ To make a hot air balloon cake, bake and ice a simple square cake. Place a straw in each corner and position a balloon in the middle of the straws.

## TRAIN INVITATIONS AND REPLY CARDS

*Stiff paper (30 cm (12 in) wide*
*Felt tip pens or crayons*

1. Fold paper into 3, concertina fashion. Lay it down so that the first fold is on the right hand side, the second on the left hand side.
2. Draw a simple train shape across the width of the paper. A rectangle for the body, square for the cab, circles for the wheels.
3. Cut out the train, taking care not to cut along the folds.
4. Open out the card, on the second train write the details of the party. On the last train, write 'I can/cannot come to the party'.

You can really cheat at making a train birthday cake by using a chocolate swiss roll, mini rolls and chocolate biscuits.

## FARMYARD ANIMAL INVITATIONS AND REPLY CARDS

*Stiff pink paper*
*Pink gift wrap ribbon (the sort that can be curled over the blade of a pair of scissors)*
*Felt tip pens or crayons*
*Staple gun and staples*

1. Fold stiff paper in half and place with the fold at the top.
2. Draw a simple pig shape. Begin by drawing a large oval with the top against the fold of the paper. Inside the oval, draw a circle for the head, an oval for the snout, two triangles for the ears, two more for the front trotters and two small circles for the eyes.
3. Cut out the pig shape leaving at least 3 cm (1¼ in) of the fold uncut. The pig should be

capable of standing up.

4. Inside the card, write the details of the party.

5. Curl a short length of ribbon over the blade of a pair of scissors and staple it to the back of the card to resemble the pig's curly tail – obviously

☆ To make a farmyard cake, simply use green butter-cream or roll out icing and decorate with a few toy farm animals.

## CLOCK PARTY INVITATIONS

*Stiff coloured paper*
*Felt tip pens or crayons*

1. Using a small saucer or cup as a template, draw around and cut out as many circles of papers as invitations needed.

2. Using pens or crayons, help child to fill in the clock face and the party details, setting the clock at the time the party begins. Set the dial at the party date and give the venue to resemble the clock manufac-turer's name and address.

If you are making a clock birthday cake, set the hands at the same number as the age of the birthday girl or boy.

If, like me, you would like to strangle the person who introduced 'party bags', but hate the idea of disappointing the 'birthday boy' or 'girl', wrap a few sweets in some pretty lace or chiffon for the girls and in toilet roll crackers for the boys. Alternatively, fill a bucket with some sawdust or polystyrene chips and let every child have a 'lucky dip' gift to go home with.

# RHYMES AND SONGS

If we think about it we probably all know dozens of rhymes and children's songs. Isn't it amazing then how often we cannot remember a single 'ditty' when put on the spot! Here are a few traditional rhymes and songs. Most you will know, some you will have probably forgotten!

Rhymes and songs widen the vocabulary, and help develop confidence and concentration. They may well introduce numbers to a child and sharing a few rhymes and songs can be soothing and reassuring or offer an opportunity to 'let rip' and use up some excess energy.

## TRADITIONAL NURSERY RHYMES

Here are a few old favourites that you may enjoy remembering from your own childhood.

### *SING A SONG OF SIXPENCE*

Sing a song of sixpence
A pocket full of rye
Four and twenty blackbirds
baked in a pie

When the pie was opened
The birds began to sing
Wasn't that a dainty dish
to set before the king?

The King was in the counting
                house
        counting out his money
    The Queen was in the parlour
        eating bread and honey

    The maid was in the garden
        hanging out the clothes
when down came a blackbird
        and pecked off her nose.

### JACK AND JILL

    Jack and Jill went up the hill
        to fetch a pail of water
    Jack fell down and broke his crown
    And Jill came tumbling after

    Up Jack got and home did trot
        as fast as he could caper
    They put him to bed and wrapped his head
    With vinegar and brown paper.

### MARY, MARY, QUITE CONTRARY

    Mary, Mary, Quite contrary,
    how does your garden grow?
With silver bells and cockle shells
    and pretty maids all in a row.

## *HUMPTY DUMPTY*

Humpty Dumpty sat on a wall
Humpty Dumpty had a great fall
All the King's horses and all the King's men
couldn't put Humpty together again.

## *BAA BAA BLACK SHEEP*

Baa Baa black sheep,
have you any wool?
Yes Sir, yes Sir,
three bags full

One for my master and
one for my dame
And one for the little boy
who lives down the lane.

## *I HAD A LITTLE NUT TREE*

I had a little nut tree
Nothing did it bear,
but a silver nutmeg
and a golden pear
The King of Spain's daughter
came to visit me
And all for the sake of my
little nut tree.

### *OLD KING COLE*

Old King Cole was a merry old soul,
and a merry old soul was he
He called for his pipe and he called for his glass
and he called for his fiddlers three

Every fiddler had a fine fiddle,
and a very fine fiddle had he
Twee tweedle dee, tweedle dee went the fiddlers
Oh! there's none so rare as can compare
with King Cole and his fiddlers three!

## ACTION RHYMES

Children quickly pick up the actions that go with the rhymes. Most children like showing off a little and action rhymes such as these are good confidence builders. The actions in these songs are all fairly self-explanatory.

### *I'M AS TALL AS A HOUSE*

I'm as tall as a house
I'm as small as a mouse
I'm as straight as a pin
With my tummy tucked in!

## WIDE-EYED OWL

There's a wide-eyed owl
  With a pointed nose
   Slits for his ears
And claws for his toes.

   He sits in a tree
   And looks at you
   He flaps his wings
And says 'Twit Twoo'.

## I'M A LITTLE TEAPOT

I'm a little teapot
Short and stout
Here's my handle
Here's my spout
When I hear the teacups
Hear me shout
'Tip me up and pour me out!'

## JACK IN A BOX

Jack in a Box jumps up like this
And he makes me laugh as he
     waggles his head
I gently press him down again
Saying 'Jack in a Box' you must go
        to bed.

### *AN ELEPHANT GOES LIKE THIS AND LIKE THAT*

An elephant goes like this and like
  that
He's terribly tall and he's terribly
  fat
He has no fingers, he has no toes
But goodness gracious — what a
  long nose!

> You know the chil-
> dren are ready for
> something more
> sophisticated when
> they look at you as if
> you were the child
> and tell you that an
> elephant has a trunk,
> not a nose!

### *JUMP UP AND DOWN TO EXERCISE*

I can rub my elbows
I can pat my eyes
I can jump up and down to
  exercise!

I can rub my tummy
I can pat my thighs
I can jump up and down to
  exercise!

## *MISS POLLY*

Miss Polly had a dolly who was
   sick, sick, sick
So she 'phoned for the doctor to
   come quick, quick, quick
The doctor came with his bag and
   his hat
And he knocked at the door with a
   rat-a-tat-tat
He looked at the dolly and he
   shook his head
And he said 'Miss Polly, put her
   straight to bed'
He wrote on the paper for a pill,
   pill, pill
And said, 'I'll be back in the
   morning with my bill, bill, bill.'

## *I HAD A LITTLE*

## *CHERRY STONE*

I had a little cherry stone
I put it in the ground
And when I came to look at it
A tiny shoot I found
The shoot grew up and up each
   day
And soon became a tree
I picked the juicy cherries
and I ate them for my tea!

### THE TREE

Here is the tree with its leaves so
  green
Here are the apples that hang in
  between
When the wind blows the apples
  fall
Here is the basket to gather them
  all.

## NUMBER RHYMES

Number rhymes can be counted on fingers or 'pretend'
buns, or whatever is handy. If you have enough
children they enjoy joining in the action: buying the
buns, hopping into the pool, and so on.

### FIVE LITTLE SQUIRRELS

Five little squirrels sitting in a tree
The first one said 'What do I see?'
The second one said 'A man with
  a gun'
The third one said 'Let's run,
  run, run'.
The fourth one said 'Let's hide
  in the shade'.
The fifth one said 'I'm not afraid'.
Then 'bang' went the gun and
  away they all ran!

### *FIVE CURRANT BUNS*
### *IN THE BAKER'S SHOP*

Five currant buns in the baker's
  shop
Big and round with sugar on top
Along came (*choose someone's
  name*) with a penny one day
Bought a currant bun and took it
  away.

Four currant buns in the baker's
  shop . . . .
  (*repeat with three, two, one*)

No currant buns in the baker's
  shop
Big and round with sugar on top
Along came – – – – – – with a
  penny one day
'Sorry', said the baker, 'no buns left
  today'.

### *ONE, TWO, THREE, FOUR, FIVE*

One, two, three, four, five
Once I caught a fish alive
Six, seven, eight, nine, ten
Then I let him go again.
Why did you let it go?
Because it bit my finger so.
Which finger did it bite?
This little finger on the right!

## FIVE LITTLE SPECKLED FROGS

Five little speckled frogs sat on a
    speckled log
Eating the most delicious grubs –
    glub, glub
One jumped into the pool
Where it was nice and cool
Then there were four speckled
    frogs – glub, glub

Four little speckled frogs sat on a
    speckled log . . .
    (*repeat with three and two*)

One little speckled frog sat on a
    speckled log
Eating the most delicious grubs –
    glub, glub
Then he jumped into the pool
Where it was nice and cool
Then there were no more speckled
    frogs – glub, glub.

### *PETER HAMMERS WITH*
### *ONE HAMMER*

Peter hammers with one hammer,
  one hammer, one hammer
  (*tap with one fist*)
Peter hammers with one hammer
  this fine day.
Peter hammers with two hammers,
  two hammers, two hammers ...
  (*repeat with two, three, four,
  and five hammers, two fists,
  feet and head*)

Peter's fast asleep now, sleep now,
  sleep now
Peter's fast asleep now this fine
  day.
  (*rest head on hands to sleep*)

Peter's wide awake now, wake
  now, wake now
Peter's wide awake now this fine day.
  (*tap all five 'hammers' again!*)

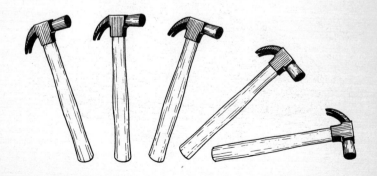

### FIVE LITTLE DUCKS WENT

Five little ducks went out one day
Over the hills and far away
Mother duck said 'Quack, Quack,
    Quack, Quack'
And four little ducks came
    swimming back.

Four little ducks went out one day
Over the hills and far away ...
    (*repeat with three, two, one*)

Mother duck went out one day
Over the hills and far away
Mother duck said 'Quack, Quack,
    Quack, Quack'
And five little ducks came
    swimming back.

## SONGS

I used to sing these songs when I was little. Many of
them have actions to follow and they are all fun to sing.

### HEAD AND SHOULDERS

Head, shoulders, knees and toes
Knees and toes
Head, shoulders, knees and toes
Knees and toes
And eyes and ears and mouth and
    nose
Head and shoulders, knees and
    toes, knees and toes.

## I HEAR THUNDER

I hear thunder.
I hear thunder.
Hark, don't you?
Hark, don't you?
Pitter, patter raindrops,
Pitter, patter raindrops,
I'm wet through.
So are you.

I see blue skies.
I see blue skies.
Way up high.
Way up high.
Hurry up the sunshine,
Hurry up the sunshine.
I'll soon dry.
So will you.

## OATS AND BEANS
## AND BARLEY GROW

Oats and beans and barley grow,
Oats and beans and barley grow,
But you, nor I, nor anyone knows
How oats and beans and barley grow.

First the farmer sows the seeds
Then stands back and takes his ease
Stamps the ground and claps his
    hands
Then turns around to survey his
    lands.

## IN A COTTAGE

In a cottage in a wood,
A little man at the window stood,
Saw a rabbit running by,
Knocking at the door.
'Help me! Help me! Help me! he said,
'Before the hunter shoots me dead'.
'Come little rabbit, come with me,
Happy we shall be!'

## IF YOU ARE HAPPY
## AND YOU KNOW IT

*This is my favourite children's song. You can really raise the roof with this one. Ask the children for their suggestions for actions: 'If you're happy and you know it, jump up high.'*

If you're happy and you know it
Clap your hands
If you're happy and you know it
Clap your hands.
If you're happy and you know it
And you really want to show it
If you're happy and you know it
Clap your hands.

*Second verse* Stamp your feet

*Third verse* Nod your head

*Fourth verse* Shout 'I am'.

*Simple tongue twisters can be fun to try. Make up some easy ones: 'Daring Dan dived deep down' or attempt the almost impossible 'She sells sea shells by the sea shore'.*

### *TWINKLE, TWINKLE*
### *LITTLE STAR*

Twinkle, twinkle little star
How I wonder what you are
Up above the world so high
Like a diamond in the sky!

### *UNDER THE COVERS*

Under the covers,
Eyes shut tight.
May happy dreams be with you
All through the dark night.

And in the morning,
When the light peeps through.
May it welcome the day
Those dreams all come true!

# INDEX

## THE FAMILY MATTERS SERIES